BUSINESS SUCCESS THROUGH RISK ELIMINATION

BUSINESS SUCCESS THROUGH RISK ELIMINATION

The Top Ten Rules of Successful Start-Ups

BRIAN DAVIES

iUniverse, Inc.
Bloomington

BUSINESS SUCCESS THROUGH RISK ELIMINATION
The Top Ten Rules of Successful Start-Ups

Copyright © 2010, 2013 by Brian Davies.

All rights reserved. No part of this book may be used or reproduced by any means, graphic, electronic, or mechanical, including photocopying, recording, taping or by any information storage retrieval system without the written permission of the publisher except in the case of brief quotations embodied in critical articles and reviews.

iUniverse books may be ordered through booksellers or by contacting:

iUniverse
1663 Liberty Drive
Bloomington, IN 47403
www.iuniverse.com
1-800-Authors (1-800-288-4677)

Because of the dynamic nature of the Internet, any web addresses or links contained in this book may have changed since publication and may no longer be valid. The views expressed in this work are solely those of the author and do not necessarily reflect the views of the publisher, and the publisher hereby disclaims any responsibility for them.

Any people depicted in stock imagery provided by Thinkstock are models, and such images are being used for illustrative purposes only.
Certain stock imagery © Thinkstock.

ISBN: 978-1-4759-7143-9 (sc)
ISBN: 978-1-4759-7145-3 (hc)
ISBN: 978-1-4759-7144-6 (ebk)

Printed in the United States of America

iUniverse rev. date: 02/13/2013

CONTENTS

Introduction vii

Part One: Finance
Reduce Your Risk with Solid Financial Strategies

Rule #10   Equity Financing:
                 A Step toward Start-Up Success 3
Rule #9   Line of Credit: Your Safety Net 9
Rule #8   Accurate Financial Models 14
Rule #7   Controlling Expenses: A Crucial Step 19
Rule #6   Sales: The Key to Success 26

Part Two: Management and Planning
Reduce Your Risk with Effective Systems and Planning

Rule #5   The Sales and Marketing Plan 37
Rule #4   Business Ethics and Integrity 45
Rule #3   Roles and Responsibilities 50
Rule #2   Your Area of Experience and Expertise 56
Rule #1   Success through Determination 60

Afterword 63
Glossary 69
Bibliography 71
About the Author 73

INTRODUCTION

Starting a business does not have to be risky.

Let me repeat that: starting a business does not have to be risky. This book will show you how to minimize the risk of starting a business by learning the specific techniques that successful entrepreneurs use. You will see how to manage risk so that you have the confidence needed to make the leap from employee to business owner. Once you learn to manage risk, you can virtually eliminate it.

There is no magic to starting a successful start-up business. It is hard but doable. Based on my experience, there are very specific traits that nearly all successful start-up companies have in common. The presence or lack of these ten traits marks the distinction between successful start-up companies and those that end in bankruptcy. If you can successfully manifest these ten traits, you will virtually guarantee your start-up business success.

Entrepreneurs put their money into a project or a business and risk losing everything. This book will show you that risk can be controlled and dramatically reduced. You can control this risk by learning from those who went before you, by learning what works and what doesn't. Starting a business shouldn't be like a Hail Mary pass in football. Rather it is a calculated risk and managed risk. With the proper planning and education, you can significantly improve your chances for having a successful start-up business.

According to the Small Business Administration, more than fifty percent of all start-up business fail within the first five years of operation. You can and should use the experiences of entrepreneurs before you to help you avoid this fate. Since untold numbers of people have traveled down the same business road you are about to travel down, why shouldn't you learn from their successes and failures? You can minimize your risk by letting their experiences guide you. Why reinvent the wheel? Throughout this book, I have inserted real-life examples from my own experience and the experiences of some of my entrepreneurial colleagues. Take the best practices from start-up successes and avoid the pitfalls of start-up failures.

In 1995 my partner and I incorporated a start-up manufacturing business in the medical device market. We sold the business in 2006 to a large publicly traded company, the Brady Corporation (NYSE: BRC). Throughout these ten years we had some great successes and some major setbacks. For example, one of our first setbacks came shortly after we launched when our initial sales forecast was based on a sales plan that did not work out. The problem was that we did not have a back-up sales plan. So now I recommend building your sales plan based on your most accurate projections, but you also need a fall back plan, or Plan B, if your primary plan does not work out. My hope is that you will use the lessons of business owners with successful start-ups and learn from our successes and failures.

By reading this book, you'll gain valuable insight into distinctions that can help to make your start-up venture a success. These distinctions are a *top ten* of vital factors in your success. The "Financial" part of the book focuses on financial strategies, and you'll learn how to sensibly use equity financing, manage sales growth, control your expenses, model key financial indicators, and secure a line of credit. In the "Planning and Management" part, you'll learn how to develop a business plan, manage your business with integrity, manage personnel, develop your area of expertise, and have faith and determination in your success. You'll read real-life case studies about entrepreneurs just like you who have overcome challenges along the way to business success.

No one is born an entrepreneur. Being an entrepreneur is a choice. Being an entrepreneur is using a set of skills that are learned and refined, often by trial and error. You have the opportunity to learn from entrepreneurs who came before you. Just as important, you can learn what not to do. By doing this, you reduce the risk associated with starting your own business. Whether you are starting a manufacturing business or a retail business, expanding your service operation, contracting as a freelance provider, or doing any entrepreneurial activity, this book will help you make wise, crucial decisions that reduce risk. With this book, you have the opportunity to learn the differences between successful start-up businesses and start-up failures.

The premise of this book is this: *you can reduce and nearly eliminate the risk of starting your business.* I'll show you how in the next chapters.

Part One

FINANCE

*Reduce Your Risk
with Solid Financial Strategies*

Rule #10

EQUITY FINANCING: A STEP TOWARD START-UP SUCCESS

Expect the unexpected when you start a business from scratch.

Rule #10

Start-up successes use equity financing.
Start-up failures use too much debt financing.

There are two types of business financing you can use when you start your business. One is debt, and the other is equity. They reside on opposite ends of the risk spectrum. Start-up successes use **equity financing**—the less risky money. Start-up failures use too much **debt financing.**

Equity financing is the foundation of a successful new business. This is money that is put into the business by the owners and other shareholders. The people who put this type of money into the company own a piece of the company. Some of the typical sources of this type money are the owners, relatives, venture capital companies, and other business partners. This money is not a loan; it is repaid in the form of stock and dividends.

Debt financing is money put into the company in the form of a loan. These loans typically come from a lending institution like a bank or the Small Business Administration (SBA), via your local bank. This money is paid back usually on a monthly basis. This money is a debt for the company and is paid back out of cash from business activities. Because debt financing must be paid every month, it is a burden on the company and increases the start-up risk.

> ### Case Study
>
> In the first six months of my first start-up, we encountered several obstacles and unplanned events. Our business was started in 1995 as a contract manufacturer in the health-care industry. Our business plan was based in large part on sales to a company with whom we had personal relationships. It was outsourcing the manufacturing for its consumer retail product.
>
> Two months into the business our customer informed us it was reducing the number of suppliers from five to two. We were not one of the two. This had an enormous impact on our plan. This one customer/prospect represented about 50 percent of our projected sales in year one. Suddenly our sales were short of plan; it was the worst-case scenario. Sales were slow to ramp up and were behind plan for most of the first year. Because of this, our revenues dropped but our expenses did not change. If our business financing had relied too heavily on debt, our cash flow and business would have been in immediate trouble.

This example illustrates the type of unexpected and unplanned events that can occur and the havoc they can create in your new business. The important distinction between equity financing and debt financing is that equity financing isn't a monthly drain on cash flow. It enables you to absorb unexpected events more easily. Debt financing is a loan with a scheduled repayment plan, usually monthly. This loan (debt) will usually come from a bank, the SBA, or another institution. If your revenues suddenly drop, you still have to make this loan payment. This drains cash from your business. And because cash flow is the lifeblood of any business, it is important to maintain the integrity of cash flow at all times.

Equity financing eliminates this payment burden. With equity financing you raise money by selling a part of your company in exchange for ownership (equity). This lump-sum cash infusion is used to pay expenses of the company while sales and profits are being built. When the company receives this type money, it is an investment by the person, institution, or group in the business. This money is not paid back on a scheduled payment plan so it does not drain cash and create a burden on cash flow. The equity investor expects to see the return of the money invested plus growth, usually over several years. Often the equity investors are paid back when the company is sold.

Whether you use equity or debt financing or a combination of the two, make sure you get enough money in the beginning. As a general rule, you should have enough money to take you through your worst-case business/sales plan. You will know the level of financing is adequate when your cash-flow model stays positive—that is, it does not run out of money. As you start the task of building your business, it is very disruptive to have to stop and go back to the activity of raising additional money.

One tool that will help you determine how much money/capital you need to finance your business is to build a cash-flow statement. You can find standard cash-flow statements in an Excel spreadsheet on the Internet or in the business section of the bookstore. This spreadsheet will use sales and expense projections that model your cash flow. How much money or cash will you be bringing in from customers and how much cash will be outgoing from your operating expenses? You should build your cash-flow model based on your most accurate projections, Plan A, and your back-up, Plan B. The cash in your bank account must last until profits are sufficient to enable the business to operate on its own.

Case Study

Our next unplanned event nearly resulted in an uncollectable account receivable invoice of $50,000 to one of our new customers. As a supplier of disposable medical devices and components, one of the products we supplied was an antifog plastic eye shield that our customer used to make its hospital surgical mask. On a hot July day, we made a large shipment of these shields from our plant in Texas. The plastic shields became stuck together during the hot and humid truck shipment. There was a question from our customer's receiving quality personnel regarding whether or not they would even be able to use the shields. If not, we would be facing a product reject and an uncollectable invoice of $50,000. Would we be able to recover from a cash-flow hit of that magnitude? Meanwhile, our payment to our raw material supplier was still due even if our customer rejected the shipment.

When it comes to equity financing, most entrepreneurs want to hold onto as much ownership of their companies as they can. This is the primary reason they use debt financing. The problem with this approach surfaces when the unexpected happens to your business and plan. If your plan suddenly starts down the *worst-case* path, will your cash flow survive? If your cash flow does not survive, neither will your business. There is a balancing act between debt and equity financing. More debt financing allows you to hold onto more ownership of your company, but with increased risk.

There is a place for both debt and equity financing in most businesses. The ratio between the two differs from business to business and industry to industry. Your bankers, financial advisors, and investors will give you a good idea about what this ratio might be for your situation.

Remember that it's better to have less ownership in a successful start-up business than more ownership in a start-up failure.

One strategy is to plan your finances so that you can survive for one year (rent, food, etc.) without any income from the new business. If you can implement this strategy without burdensome debt, your new business will be off to a great start and this will substantially enhance your chances for success.

One last note on business financing: there is a little known creative financing secret that can be used to finance your business and retain the most equity possible. It is by entering a joint venture (JV) with another company. This can be a powerful method that benefits both parties. Here is how it works: You *give away* a certain percentage ownership in your company in exchange for support in the early years of your business. For example, your JV partner will be an established business with infrastructure you can use. Your JV partner will pay salaries, provide office space, warehouse space, accounting services, etc. The exchange of equity for this support can take on an almost endless number of varieties. The benefit of this type arrangement is that some of the support isn't truly an added or new expense on your JV partner.

As an example, in another start-up I was involved with we "traded" equity in our company for salary support for a key individual and free rent; both lasted three years. Not having these two burdensome expenses kept our expenses (overhead) as low as possible. This made it much easier to attain profitability. Your partner company already has a building, warehouse, accounting employees, etc. You will simply use those assets and resources that are already being used by your JV partner. You use this support until your new business gets to break-even.

Financing Summary

- Debt financing is a loan with regular payments that affect cash flow.
- Equity financing is selling part of the business ownership for later dividends; there are no regular monthly payments.
- When starting out, plan on having a minimum of one year's personal expenses set aside so that the business cash flow can be maintained without owner salary.
- Consider a joint venture equity financing to get started.

Rule #9

LINE OF CREDIT: YOUR SAFETY NET

Rule #9

Start-up successes have a secure line of credit.
Start-up failures do not have a line of credit.

Start-up successes have a preapproved **line of credit** (LOC) to use in their business from day one. This is put in place before it is needed.

Cash flow is the lifeblood of any business. Your line of credit allows you to manage cash flow to the optimal benefit of your company. A business line of credit is a prearranged loan from a lending institution that you pull from and pay back regularly. With the tight credit markets today, obtaining a line of credit may be a tough task to accomplish for a start-up business. However, it is more important today than ever before to help you navigate this economy.

Start-up failures make the mistake of starting their business without a line of credit in place. This is dangerous and is like learning to walk a high wire without a net below you. Your LOC is your cash-flow safety net. What would happen to your business if a large customer suddenly couldn't pay its bill? Could you survive that? What if routine accounts receivable don't come in as quickly as you planned, or if you experience more bad debt than planned? If you have your line of credit in place, you can pull the funds from your LOC to bridge your cash-flow gap. Poor cash flow is the single biggest risk factor for your new business. It is what keeps entrepreneurs up at night and negative cash flow for too long will drive you out of business.

> Your LOC is the safety net under your cash flow plan.

There are many normal everyday business situations that will fuel your need for a LOC.

- Slow accounts receivable
- Bad debt
- Rapid sales growth
- Unexpected expenses

There are others, and it is likely that you will have to deal with all of these situations early on in your business. Be prepared.

Successful start-ups have a prearranged line of credit in place and ready to use. In most cases, the owner will be required to sign a personal guarantee for the debt. This is not new and is not a result of the current tight credit market. Personal guarantees have always been a fundamental banking requirement for most new business loans.

Case Study

In our business, we arranged for two lines of credit from two different banks. Both were based on personal guarantees and both banks offered the same amount of $25,000. So now we had a $50,000 safety net under our business. If you have good credit and a good business plan, you should be able to secure a small LOC.

It is best to set up your LOC before you open your doors for business. If this is not possible, you should secure one as soon as you can. Keep a close relationship with your banker. Get to know him or her. Invite him into your business. Send him monthly and quarterly financial statements so he is aware of your business. Take the time to go to lunch with your banker. He is a key part of your success and team.

The time to ask for and apply for a LOC is when you don't need it. Banks vary in their attitudes toward small and start-up businesses. You will have to interview several bankers to find the right fit. Early in your business, you may have extra cash in the bank. Go get the LOC then. If you wait until cash is tight and you have a real need for a short-term loan, your banker will perceive that as being much more risky than if you had applied for it before the real need was there.

Maybe you have seen the phrase "Happiness is positive cash flow." Until you attain that *happiness*, your LOC can be your best friend.

Your objective is to have cash flowing so nicely that you don't need to tap your LOC. Even if you don't need to use your LOC, it is a good practice to borrow from it anyway, pay it back, and repeat this. If you do not use your LOC you will lose it. When a bank gives you a LOC, it is tying up that amount of money as if it was lending it to you. If you don't pull from your LOC and allow the bank to lend its money to you and make money on this loan, then it will pull back this reserve for you and use it for more profitable purposes.

Alternatives to LOCs

Credit is very tight today. If the banks refuse your LOC applications, you can turn to credit cards. Most major credit cards come with a cash advance feature, which is essentially a personal line of credit. It is much more expensive than money from your local bank, but it can be nice to have. This credit card LOC can also be used in addition to your bank LOC. As mentioned earlier, one last angle to work is to secure an LOC at more than one bank. Banks evaluate each person and business individually so you can have more than one LOC at a time.

There are more creative—and often more effective—ways to improve your cash flow. Customer financing and vendor financing are great methods. If your customers are other businesses (business-to-business, aka B2B sales), you typically must wait thirty days after you provide your product or service before you get paid. You can simply ask or require a customer to prepay for its purchase either in whole or part. This gives you cash immediately rather than waiting thirty days. You can offer incentives for your customers to pay early. These typically are discounts to entice them to pay in ten days instead of thirty. You can also work with your suppliers so they give you extended payment terms. Normal business-to-business payment terms are *net thirty*, where your customers pay your invoice 30 days after they receive your goods or service. If you can get your suppliers to extend your payment terms to sixty days or ninety days, you will cash-flow much more easily.

Case Study

Recently a local business acquaintance asked one of his larger packaging suppliers for ninety-day terms. He got a yes answer almost before he got the request out of his mouth. It is in your suppliers' best interest to help you succeed. This type of partnership will build long-lasting relationships. I am sure these two companies will do business together for a long time.

Your LOC is the bridge between your income statement and your cash-flow statement. Set up your line of credit before you need it. It is almost certain that you will be glad you have it to bridge your cash flow, particularly if you work with credit terms from customers or suppliers.

Line of Credit Summary

- A line of credit is a prearranged loan that allows you to access the funds when needed.
- A LOC will assist with cash flow if needed.
- Alternatives to LOCs exist: credit cards and supplier financing are two examples.

Rule #8

ACCURATE FINANCIAL MODELS

Rule #8

> **Successful start-ups have accurate cash-flow and income-statement models.**
> **Start-up failures have flaws in their financial models.**

Start-up successes have accurate financial models—especially the cash-flow and P&L models—and they use them to guide their businesses. Start-up failures have incomplete, inaccurate, unused, or flawed financial models.

Good financial planning is critical to your success and your ability to minimize start-up risk. You must know what lies ahead with your finances. Your blueprints for this are your financial statements. These include the **income statement, balance sheet, and cash-flow statement.**

For clarification, let me describe each of the tools.

income statement (profit and loss statement): measures expenses against sales revenue to show the income (or loss) to a business. It is measured over a specific period of time—like a month or year.

balance sheet: shows a financial picture of a business. It specifically shows assets, liabilities, and ownership. It is measured at a given point in time—like at year-end.

cash-flow statement: shows how cash is exchanged between the business and the outside world. It shows how cash is generated and what it is spent on.

> ### Case Study
>
> Recently, I reviewed a plan for a company that was using its cash-flow statement to forecast its need for cash. The company had assumed it would get paid from its customers thirty days from its invoice date. This is a reasonable assumption, except that it was actually taking thirty-eight days to get paid—not thirty. This cash-flow error led the company to believe it could cover its expenses by sales revenue. The extra eight days of waiting to be paid was draining its cash and making it difficult to pay its bills on time. Once the company realized this, it had to decide either to bring its accounts receivable in sooner (thirty days) or expand its line of credit at the bank to handle the gap in cash.

Another item to plan for is the volatility of commodities or your purchased raw materials. Will the rise and fall of commodity prices affect your cash flow? If so, you should plan for a worst-case scenario. A company we did business with relied on resin to manufacture its product. The company planned its business around very high resin prices when oil was at $140+ per barrel. When oil fell to $40 per barrel, its business was much more profitable. The company was able to pass on some of those "planned" cost savings to its customers and keep a significant portion for itself. You might want to build in yearly raw material price increases in your COGS (cost of goods sold) section because it is highly unlikely in today's volatile economy that any business that is based on raw material purchases can expect to have a flat COGS over time.

Your banker will be delighted to see accurate and complete financial statements. When you can accurately predict your business's need for cash, line of credit, and loans, the banks will view you as a capable financial manager. Make sure your financial models and statements are accurate and complete. This will help lower your risk and make cash management much more accurate.

Start-up failures run their businesses with flawed models. These flawed models aren't necessarily flawed because of errors. They can be miscalculations. One common area of miscalculation is sales. If you are not meeting your top-line sales numbers, it will create havoc on your financial planning models. Start-up failures neglect to make adjustments to their models when confronted with new and more accurate information. The purpose of financial models is to predict the future. Your model should be a living document. Adjust it when you are presented with new information.

Cash Flow vs. Income

There is a subtle but profound difference between the income your business generates and the **cash flow** it generates. While these two are related, they tell two different stories about your business. Of the two, cash flow is king. If your business is cash-flowing, your income statement is healthy. The reverse is not necessarily true. You can be earning a profit as shown on your income statement but not breaking even on your cash-flow statement.

Let's say you sell bicycle tires to bicycle manufacturers. You sell $15,000 of tires in one month and your cost of goods sold is

$10,000. You make $5,000 profit—right? Okay, but the bicycle manufacturer pays you in thirty days from when you ship/ and invoice. You don't have this $5,000 to spend, but it shows up on the income statement as income as soon as you invoice it. Your income statement show you have $5,000 profit to spend, but you don't—not until the cash flows into the business. If your business is growing fast, this problem is multiplied.

Income statements can be distorted by differences in accounting practices. The cash-flow model is considered gospel by entrepreneurs and investors. It shows the movements of cash and the business requirement for cash. The cash-flow statement gives a more accurate view of the financial health of the business. As in the example above when you sell something, it counts as a sale in your income statement. For cash-flow purposes, that sale is only a potentially worthless account receivable until you collect it. Then the sale is cash, and only then is it useful to the business. This is why you can be very profitable on paper (income statement) and not able to meet your monthly expenses. Income and cash flow are not the same. On the cash-flow statement, an account receivable is not cash until it is collected. The income statement does not make this subtle but profound distinction.

> Manage your cash movements and cash health via your cash flow statement and keep it up to date.

When planning the cash needs of your business, rely only on the cash-flow model. It will show the true cash needs of the business. Of course you will need to be able to show your business is able to make a profit via your income statement, but in order to pay the expenses of your business you must have the cash in the bank. Lastly, if you see your business is running tight on cash, take immediate action to fix this. You can take a variety of actions, like tightening up your invoice collections, offering discounts for your customers to pay early, or arranging for a line of credit at your bank.

Accurate Financial Models Summary

- The income statement, balance sheet, and cash-flow statements are the blueprint for your business success.
- Each statement serves a different purpose for analyzing a business's financial health.
- Your accountant and banker will have the most input and interest in these statements. Keep them up-to-date and accurate.

Rule #7

CONTROLLING EXPENSES: A CRUCIAL STEP

Rule #7

**Start-up successes control their expenses.
Start-up failures have expenses that are too high.**

Regardless of how good your business plan is, you will incur unforeseen expenses. A key distinction between success and failure is that start-up successes control their expenses, while start-up failures have expenses that are too high. Successful companies manage their expenses according to their business plans.

Your Threshold to Profitability

Some expenses can be controlled. For example, do you really need the latest laptop computer or will a used one do the same job? What about the leather chair and new desk? Expenses drain cash from the business. Expenses that are too high can kill cash flow. By keeping your expenses as low as possible, you are making it easier for your business to generate positive cash flow. And every entrepreneur knows that *happiness is positive cash flow.*

> Keep your expenses and
> overhead as low as possible.

> **Case Study**
>
> In an effort to keep our expenses low, we used a number of creative tactics. For example, during the early years of our business we had one used computer and used tables instead of desks. When we travelled, we stayed two people to a room. You can negotiate everything you spend money on. You should spend your money on expense items that are going to grow your business. So staying at a budget hotel is preferable to staying at a five-star hotel. We made it as easy as possible to be profitable. Keep your overhead and expenses as low as possible in the early years of the business and make it that much easier to attain positive cash flow.

I have seen entrepreneur after entrepreneur be too concerned with looking good. Typically, they have the company pay for their new car, they stay at the expensive hotel rather than a budget hotel, and their offices have new and expensive furniture and equipment. The end result is a drain of cash that leads to the end of the business or at minimum another round of financing to pay for these items.

What happens if expenses are double your plan? If sales are on plan but expenses are high, will your business survive? Review your cash flow plan thoroughly. With one start-up plan I reviewed, the electric utility expense was underestimated by $1,000 per month. This simple error had a significant impact on cash flow. As mentioned previously, keep expenses as low as you can: double up on hotel rooms, keep salaries as low as possible, especially for employees who are owners, and cut all unnecessary expenses to the bone. High-end furniture, desks, copiers, and equipment are not necessary unless you have frequent meetings with customers and prospects in your office, and even then you can still avoid this expense by utilizing the many office rental executive suites by the day, by the month, or longer. To find this type of short term office space simply do an Internet search on "executive suites."

What is your business's threshold to profitability? Is it as low as it can be?

Where you can, you should consider outsourcing parts of your business in order to control expenses. For instance, if your industry requires a quality system that is ISO (International Standards Organization) certified, you can outsource that function rather than hire a direct employee with a large and burdensome salary. Payroll would be another example of an area of your company where you can outsource the entire function and save money.

Virtual Companies

It is important to keep the costs of running your day-to-day business as low as possible. The lower these *fixed*, costs the easier it will be to make a profit. There are many creative ways to lower the cost of running your business. *Virtual companies* are on the rise all over the world. These are entities that outsource everything. This approach isn't applicable to every business situation, but if it fits your model it would be well worth considering.

You might be surprised to know that some common retail and medical products are brought to market by virtual companies. In one such instance, our company supplied the product—a medical device—to a virtual company. The company had two owners and one full-time accountant/customer service employee. The owners worked out of their home in California. The payroll was even outsourced. As a contract manufacturing company, we were happy to manufacture the product for them. We even shipped the product to their customer's distribution centers. Being a virtual company allowed the owners to concentrate their efforts on sales and product development, and it kept overhead to a minimum.

Another way to save money is to lease office space temporarily. There are facilities in all major US cities that will lease conference rooms and offices by the hour, day, week, or month. You can project a very modern and professional image for a fraction of the cost of setting up your own office. These temporary office facilities offer a range of services like telephone answering, mail and parcel shipping, secretarial service, etc.

Colocate

Another creative way to keep your fixed costs down is to colocate with another company. Ideally, this other company would be more established than you and in a related business but not directly competitive. For instance, if your new business is to set up computer networks and provide IT services, you might consider colocating with a computer repair shop. Since it is already paying for rent, utilities, insurance, and similar fixed costs, it will likely be receptive to your offer to offset some of those expenses by paying for a small portion of rent and utilities. This approach will be much less expensive than buying or leasing your own facility. Colocating also has the added benefit of keeping your fixed costs or overhead as flexible as possible in the event your business situation changes. You can typically get out of a deal of this type much more easily than you can your own lease.

Joint Venture

This may well be the most effective and creative way to keep your expenses low and retain as much equity in your new venture as you can. For our purposes, a joint venture is a legal agreement between two entities to work together under a set of predetermined rules. This type arrangement can be entered into instead of raising money on the open market or from your family and friends. Whether you choose to launch your business with outside capital or a JV, you will give up ownership. Joint ventures enable you to keep more ownership than you would by raising money on the open market through a Private Placement. Each company gives value and gets value. The new company will give partial ownership (equity) in exchange for the more established company paying some of the expenses of the new company.

One of the most burdensome expenses for start-up companies is salaries. To grow your business and attract top level people, you will have to pay salaries. In a JV, you can arrange for those salaries to be paid by your partner company for a set period of time. Another large expense item for a new company is rent. Can your JV company pay your rent, or, better yet, can you colocate with them? The specifics of a JV partnership agreement are only limited by your creativity and willingness to think outside the box. Can you colocate with your JV partner? Can you offer some service by you or any of your employees to your JV partner? The possibilities are endless. The expense and risk-reduction benefits can be the leverage you need to make your venture a success.

> **Case Study**
>
> A friend of mine is the founder of a medical device company and was struggling to take his company to the next level. He decided to look for a JV partner. He found a willing company in his hometown. This partner provided support so he had more resources at his disposal. The JV deal was structured to benefit both companies.
>
> The start-up company received:
>
> - A clean room to locate equipment
> - Salary support for three years
> - Office support for accounts receivable
> - Warehouse and shipping support
> - Equipment purchases.
>
> The established company received:
>
> - Minority equity in the start-up
> - Entrée into the growth market of medical devices.

Start-up failures do not pay enough attention to day-to-day expenses or fixed costs. New entrepreneurs can get caught up with looking good and forget their primary reason for being in business. Don't be enticed by the new furniture, new cars, fancy hotels, and a nice facility. Keep your expenses down. You will have to put off instant gratification for future success. There will be a time in the life of your business when you will have a new desk and stay at a five-star hotel. That time is not in the start-up phase.

Controlling your expenses is a critical component of business success. There are many creative ways to do lower costs. Control your variable costs and give your business the best shot at producing a positive income. Don't be tempted by the lure of a new computer or a new car paid for with company funds. Your ability to delay gratification in this area will prove to be a key to your success.

Controlling Expenses Summary

- Keeping expenses low, especially in the start-up phase, will help immensely with cash flow.
- There are numerous ways to control expenses: buy used equipment, rent office space as needed instead of year-round, and outsource when possible.
- Consider virtual company strategies, colocated, and joint ventures for ways to minimize expense.

The next chapter is concerned with the flip side of the expense coin: income and sales.

Rule #6

SALES:
THE KEY TO SUCCESS

*Build sales before anything else.
It is the lifeblood of your company.*

Rule #6

**Start-up successes have rapid sales growth.
Start-up failures have slow sales growth.**

The big unknown is sales. To be successful, your business will need to provide a good or service that people want to purchase. Fundamentally, your offering has to be something that people actually want. Don't start a business with an idea or product that you think has demand. You must *know* it has demand. If there is no market for your product or service, there will be no sales.

Sales: The Key to Growth

There are many parts of your business for which you will have a clear and accurate expectation. Rent, for instance, is an expense that you will know with certainty before you launch your business. In fact, most of your expense items will be known. The big unknown is sales. What will your sales be through the first year and outward?

One of the most important distinctions between successful start-ups and start-up failures is that the successful companies often have sales that exceed their plans. Start-up failures do not meet their sales plans. If your sales miss your plan, your revenues are less than expected and that draws down your cash. Essentially, you have to use more cash to make up the shortfall between the sales you expected and actual sales. If this occurs for too long, you may run out of cash.

Many start-up businesses struggle to attain sales quickly enough to pay for their expenses. This results in a drain on your cash. New companies struggle with low sales for many reasons.

1. The founder(s) are not focused on sales.
2. Salespeople's behaviors are not adequate to support rapid growth.
3. Marketing is ineffective.
4. There is a failure to implement a strategic sales system with accountability metrics. See revenueconsultant.com for sales procedures.
5. There is a failure to develop a unique selling proposition.
6. There is not adequate demand for your product or service.

It is uncommon for a high-growth start-up company to go out of business; think of the many Internet start-up companies that grew rapidly at first but stalled and still failed in the long run. Obviously sales is one of the most important parts of your new business. Sales below plan are a drain on cash, and when the cash is gone you have to raise more money or close the doors.

> **Case Study**
>
> In the previous chapter, I told you about the part of our sales forecast that we missed when our new customer/prospect informed us that it was reducing the number of suppliers. That event caused us to miss our sales projections in year one. We didn't run into immediate trouble on our cash-flow because we relied primarily on equity and not debt to fund our business. However the lower than expected sales revenues were draining our cash faster than planned. So by missing the top-line sales forecast, you are likely to face financial trouble down the road.

Build sales before anything else. Sales are more important than your website or other marketing tools. Put your emphasis on sales. Get out there and sell. Make it your #1 priority. Meet with customers and prospective customers. Attend industry trade events. Stir things up. Talk to people about your business. Promote yourself and your business. The lifeblood of any business is sales and the resulting cash flow. It is the reason good salespeople make high salaries. Without sales, nothing else matters. Your banker will ask to see your pro-forma income statement and study your cash flow. The top line on the income statement is sales. So make sales your top-line priority.

Your Sales Plan

You should build your sales plan (and cash-flow plan) with three scenarios:

- Best case
- Most likely case
- Worst case

The best-case plan would include hitting or slightly exceeding your top-line sales projections and not exceeding your planned expenses. The most-likely plan should have lower sales and slightly higher expenses than you think you can actually achieve, and it be your best estimate. Don't be overly optimistic or pessimistic with your projections. Your worst-case plan would have considerably lower sales and higher expenses. What does your plan look like if your worst sales projections occur? What does this do to cash flow? Can you weather this storm until sales get back on track? Will you run out of money that you need to pay your fixed obligations?

Similarly, what does your income statement and cash flow look like if your sales exceed your best sales scenario? Rapid sales growth creates an increased demand for cash. Can your business handle sales growth that is above the most-likely plan or best-case plan? While this demand for cash is obviously preferable to a cash drain due to low sales, it creates a higher than normal demand for cash that also puts a financial strain on the business. Rapid sales drain cash similarly to the way low sales do. You must be prepared for both.

Case Study

Again, using the previous example of not being approved as a supplier to a company that was one of the pillars of our first year's sales forecast, our sales were slow to ramp up in year one. By the end of the year, we had replaced this customer but the damage to our cash flow was already done. We were forced to endure months of low sales while our expenses remained the same. The result was a drain on cash that had to be fixed. In year two, we had to raise additional capital. Fortunately, my partner was skilled at this and was successful in acquiring more capital from the founders and our original outside equity investors. It is important to note here that we were proactive in putting more capital into the company. We didn't wait until

> we were out of cash and in financial trouble. If you are going to raise money for your company, it is much easier to accomplish this before you are in financial trouble.

The reality is that you are very likely to experience unforeseen events that disrupt your sales plan. It can take longer for your advertising to be effective. It can take longer to finalize a contract with a customer. I found in the medical industry that it often takes longer than planned to get the necessary approvals, whether from the government or your customer. Your top salesperson can quit. Your plan should address these hazards with your worst-case plan.

Sales Talent and Systems

Finding the right sales talent is crucial. In many start-ups, the founders are the primary salespeople. This is excellent because there is nothing more important to the business than robust and profitable sales. The founders should never take their eyes off the sales ball. The company's very existence depends on sales revenues. If you are going to acquire new sales through an employee, this should be as an additional resource to the owners' efforts. To help ensure the success of your salespeople, I recommend you implement a sales system. The system for sales should be based on sales personnel behaviors and accountability metrics.

The effectiveness of a strong selling system is like a safety net under the sales forecast.

> Strong selling effectiveness procedures (SEPs) are like a safety net under the sales forecast.

We set up a new and unique set of selling procedures for our business. The essence of the plan is that the sales system should be as detailed and accountable as the company's quality system or operations system. QA and Ops systems are based on standard operating procedures (SOPs). These SOPs are provided in written format and outline employee behaviors and thus results. Why shouldn't sales employees and their behaviors be set up the same way? By following this system, you can implement selling effectiveness procedures, or SEPs, in your new business. These SEPs are essentially a handbook of behaviors and work instructions that the sales team must follow. They cover all aspects of the selling process, from prospecting to sales scripts to standardized PowerPoint presentations and marketing pieces. The system takes the guesswork and uncertainty out of the selling process.

The sales plan should be in addition to your business plan. Just having a sales plan to follow will put you ahead of most other start-ups and significantly reduce your risk. Your investors and financial partners will be very happy to see a well-thought-out sales plan with milestones and accountability metrics. Developing an effective sales plan will be time and money well spent.

In many ways, you should create a culture of sales throughout your organization. Every person and department should be focused on serving the customer. Recently I was listening to the founder of Zappos.com, an Internet seller of shoes and other consumer products. He was relaying stories of outstanding customer service that he expects from Zappos's employees. One story was about a lady who purchased a pair of shoes. When her husband died unexpectedly, she called Zappos's customer service to return the shoes. Not only did she return the shoes, but she received sympathy flowers from a customer-centered representative of Zappos. I am sure this lady will be a loyal Zappos customer for many years to come.

Customers make the wheels of a company turn. It is the fuel in the engine. Put thought and effort into how better to attract and serve (keep) your customers. If you focus on your sales plan with accountability metrics, put a standardized selling process in place, and give the best service possible, you will grow sales and your company.

Standardize your sales process like you would any other business system. This will ensure that your sales message is consistent and effective. Another benefit to standardizing the sales process with SEPs is that you company becomes reliant on the *system* and not a person. This is important for two reasons:

1. You can't always rely on people to do what you want, how you want, and when you want.
2. Because you are relying on a system, you can hire and train less experienced salespeople and reduce your cost of sales.

McDonald's is one of the greatest *systems* businesses in the world. Its systems are the reason it can hire young and inexperienced workers and deliver the same consistent product throughout the world—every time.

Sales is the most important part of your new company. Everyone involved in the business should be acutely aware of its importance and the importance of your customers. Use your sales plan to prepare for contingencies by creating best-case, most likely case, and worst-case scenarios. Finally, to ensure your success, implement selling effectiveness procedures.

Sales Summary

- Sales is the key to your company's growth; without it, you have nothing.
- Have a sales plan in place using best-case, most likely case, and worst-case scenarios.
- Develop your sales process and have systems in place to manage the sales staff.

Part Two

MANAGEMENT AND PLANNING

*Reduce Your Risk
with Effective Systems and Planning*

Rule #5

THE SALES AND MARKETING PLAN

Rule #5

> Successful start-ups have a tightly focused sales and marketing plan.
> Start-up failures are unfocused and undisciplined in their sales and marketing plan.

Successful start-ups know who their prospective customers are and what they are selling them. Start-up failures try to be everything to everybody. Their efforts and focus are not centered on a set of business themes. They are pulled in too many directions and seem to run by the seat of their pants.

Many successful companies have a **unique selling proposition** (USP). This is a statement, much like a business's mission statement, that defines the factor(s) that differentiate the sales offering of the company. It guides and focuses the sales and marketing communications efforts.

> Find your niche and seek to own it.

The Best

Consider that you will need at least two of these three qualities in your sales offering:

- Best price
- Best product
- Best service

You might not need all three, but you'd better have at least two. I will suggest to you that best price might not be the most attractive offering. Having the best price usually means low margins. If you must have the best price because your product or service is a commodity, then you must have the lowest cost so you can attain an acceptable profit. It has been shown over and over that people and companies will pay a premium for the best, and they know that the best will cost more. If this were not true then we would not have Mercedes and Lexus and the other high-end cars.

I have found through experience that people and companies will pay a higher price to get the best product and service. In most business cases, it is preferred to offer outstanding products and services and demand a fair price that allows for fair profits.

Sales Growth (see Distinction #6)

Start-up failures acquire sales at the sheer pace of the market place. They don't have a *sales mission* or USP that sets them apart from their competition and that drives sales. They drift through, getting by with adequate sales.

W. H. Brady, founder of the Brady Corporation, said, "Develop a niche and seek to own it." The company Mr. Brady founded in 1914 is now publicly traded on the New York Stock Exchange and employs about seven thousand people throughout the world. The company is the leading supplier in its market segments. Your new company can't be everything to everyone. Understand what you can and will do best, and own that space. With our last start-up, our niche became very defined in our second year. Our company developed expertise in the manufacture, packaging, and sterilization of wound-care products. Once this niche was solidified, sales growth increased rapidly. We found a niche and then became the leader in it. We knew exactly who our sales prospects were and what they wanted. We became the most knowledgeable company in our industry.

Case Study

With our medical device start-up, our niche became very defined in our second year. Initially, our business and sales plan was to provide contract manufacturing services to the medical device OEMs. That is a broad market and not very focused. During year two, we developed expertise in the manufacturing, packaging, and sterilization of wound-care products. We began in the wound-care market with one customer and supplied it with an absorbent, non-adherent pad similar to a Telfa™ pad or gauze. We were making this dressing and shipping it bulk and non-sterile. Our customer would then take the dressings and put them into pouches to be sterilized. By talking to people who worked at the wound-care companies, we found out that there was more demand for a company that could not only manufacture the wound dressing but also package and sterilize it too. So we purchased an automated packaging machine to fill this niche. Once this niche was solidified, sales grew rapidly. We were no longer too broad in our scope of providing contract manufacturing services to the medical device companies/ OEMs. We were now able to identify exactly the companies

> that we wanted as customers simply because we knew exactly where to look. We found a niche and then became the leader in it. We knew who our sales prospects were and what they wanted. This focus also made our sales and marketing activities much more productive. We became the most knowledgeable in our industry in contract manufacturing in the wound-care segment.

The number of areas of expertise or niches should be one to four, depending on your business. Focus on developing your competitive advantage. Again, this should probably not be price. The low-cost provider often does not win unless there are compelling reasons supporting it.

Your differentiating factor(s) could be having the best sales force, having the lowest cost of goods sold (COGS) for a particular product, or having a patented product. Your USP (unique selling proposition) and business plan should begin the development of these ideas that will sustain you through the rough times.

Virtual USP

You may find it difficult to find your ultimate niche or unique selling proposition in the start-up phase. Don't let this deter you. You can own a virtual USP. For instance, let's say you want to be the best supplier of homemade pies in the country. Through your marketing, you can build a brand or image around that, even if you haven't attained that distinction yet. You can be perceived as having the best quality and taste, even though it may take you years to achieve it. Portray your business as having reached its goal, and your niche will reveal itself.

In order to create a focused advantage for your company, you should conduct your business as if you have already arrived. Use word-of-mouth advertising and publicity to generate an image for your company. Your message should be consistent and clear about the USP you are building. Image is everything with a virtual USP and it will eventually lead to success in your focus areas.

Think of common products and their unique selling propositions:

Bounty: The Quicker Picker-Upper

Commodity products, such as paper towels or toilet tissue, have similar qualities. Bounty makes its mark by saying that its product absorbs spills faster. Benefit to the customer: time savings. You get the dirty work done sooner and can get on to other more important matters.

Burger King: Have It Your Way

This builds on the premise that it's easy for a customer to request changes. Benefit to the customer: satisfaction. No hassles (for trying to change the standard burger offerings) and a hamburger that's just the way you like it.

Obviously paper towels and hamburgers are everyday commodity products. Yet these two companies have created an image and a unique selling proposition to differentiate themselves from their competition. A USP is particularly important if you are going to advertise in any type of mass media.

Marketing Communications

Whatever type of marketing you choose to do, you should employ a multipronged attack. That is, don't rely on one type of marketing to drive customers. For instance, if you plan to use a newspaper advertisement, you should supplement that with other marketing methods in case the newspaper isn't effective. You can think of this like the mighty Parthenon in ancient Greece. If one of the pillars of that building fails, the structure is still strong and effective because of the numerous other pillars. Each of your marketing programs is like a pillar in your marketing Parthenon.

The Parthenon Approach to Marketing

Be creative in your marketing pillars—employ guerrilla marketing. The following are some examples of different ways in which you can draw attention to your product or service.

- Use word of mouth.
- Join your local business organizations.
- Make a banner.
- Give some product away.

- Take advantage of e-mail marketing and social media (great for younger customers).
- Make a presentation.
- Go on a local radio show.
- Try print media (great for older customers).
- Sponsor a contest or team.
- Send a press release to your local newspaper.
- Be creative . . .

Your Company

- What is unique about you?
- What do you want to be known for?
- What do your customers want?
- If you did one or two things better than anybody in your market, what would it be?

If you can answer these questions, then you can develop a USP. It isn't important that you haven't attained your USP distinction yet, just that you are working on it and developing it. Create your image and brand your company.

In your start-up business, you have to make the most effective use of your time. By having a focused sales and marketing plan, you can avoid wasting time trying to be everything to everybody. Remember to find your niche and own it. Your focus can and should be more than one item or service area. In the early stages of your business you won't be the leader, but you can act and position your company as if it was the leader. This will create clarity and focus to your marketing and selling programs.

Sales and Marketing Plan Summary

- Find your unique selling proposition and leverage it through all of your marketing efforts.
- Marketing is a multipronged endeavor; think of a variety of efforts, not just one.
- Use guerrilla marketing techniques to position your business.

Rule #4

BUSINESS ETHICS AND INTEGRITY

If you have integrity, nothing else matters.
If you don't have integrity, nothing else matters.
—Alan K. Simpson
—U.S. Senator from Wyoming

Rule #4

Successful start-ups have a solid foundation of business ethics and integrity.
Start-up failures have questionable ethics and integrity.

Many books have been written on the topic of business ethics. It is a subject that deserves discussion and attention. Without business ethics, the whole free-market system would collapse. It is the best way to conduct business. In any relationship, honesty and integrity are paramount. Without integrity in a business, the business will usually be short-lived. Integrity begins at the top and must be in place throughout the layers of the company.

Integrity in business means having ethical behavior in all of your internal and external business transactions and communications. Integrity is being honest, reliable, and fair.

This one *distinction* can be the difference between start-up success and failure. If integrity is not there, you can be nearly certain that the life of the business will be short. Successful start-ups have a solid foundation built on honesty and integrity. Start-up failures are plagued by ethics and integrity challenges.

> **Case Study**
>
> Enron is the example most used when discussing poor business ethics. It is certain that if ethics and integrity had been in place at Enron that there would have been no scandal. Insider trading is another example of bad ethics/integrity. Good business ethics/integrity is centered on the company looking out for the best interest of all involved with the company. This includes society, customers, employees, and suppliers.

Integrity has always been important in business. This fact has never changed. We have seen the high-profile examples of companies with dishonest and unethical managers. These companies have failed and resulted in untold misery for their employees and shareholders. Integrity in your business relationship goes further than employees. It extends to your customers and suppliers. With global competition, there is simply no reason for a customer to do business with a company that has questionable integrity. Everybody wants to do business with a company and people they can trust.

> **Case Study**
>
> In 2005 one of our customers decided not to pay for a shipment of product from us. There was nothing wrong with the product and there was no reason for this action. Our customer had replaced us with another supplier and decided to take a free shipment of product because they didn't need us any longer. The resulting bad debt totaled $27,000. At this point, our business was financially stable so it wasn't an insurmountable amount at all. The result to our customer was probably more burdensome than the bad debt was to us. The bad debt on its credit report and the resulting legal action all were warning signs to our competitors not to do business with this company or at a minimum to require payment in advance. This unethical company is still in business, but it is paying a high price for its unethical behavior.

In recent research performed by the Institute of Business Ethics (www.ibe.org.uk), an organization that is among the world's leaders in promoting ethical best practices for corporations, it was found that companies displaying a "clear commitment to ethical conduct" almost invariably outperform companies that do not display ethical conduct. The director of the Institute of Business Ethics, Philippa Foster Black, stated, "Not only is ethical behavior in the business world the right and principled thing to do, but it has been proven that ethical behavior pays off in financial returns." These findings deserve to be considered as an important tool for companies striving for long-term prospects and growth.

Without a doubt, you will face difficult decisions and challenges with your new business. There may be personal and personnel conflicts; there will be stress and tensions if cash flow gets tight. The last thing you want to worry about is the honesty and integrity of your business partners. I was fortunate in that respect because, even though we had our share of conflicts and challenges, we never had to waste time, energy, or money on ethics or honesty issues. I have seen young companies spend tremendous amounts of money on attorneys, which would have been needless if the owners all had integrity.

There are obvious situations you can avoid to take the lure away from someone whose ethics might be easily compromised. One customer of ours had a young lady handling both accounts receivable and accounts payable. In other words, she was the person who took in the money from customers and wrote the checks for payroll and suppliers. After a couple of years in this dual role, it was found that she had set up a dummy account and was paying that account—skimming money from the company. This illegal activity went on for over one year before the founder found out and put a stop to it. Fortunately, in this instance my friend's company didn't fail, but when you have employees who have poor ethics it can lead to many problems for your company. It can easily be the cause of start-up failure.

Business ethics are being discussed inside companies and at business schools. Universities are integrating the topic of ethics into their core classes. There are ethics classes in many business schools. With the demise of Enron and other ethically challenged businesses, there is a new emphasis on conducting business with sound ethics.

Business decisions often require choices about doing what is in the best interest of the company. When you're an entrepreneur, the choice is often between *you* and *the business*. With this choice, make it a point to *do the right thing*—regardless of the consequences to the business. In the long run, taking the ethical path will turn out to be the best for the business. Simply put, you get out of the business what you put in. The question of business ethics really boils down to the age-old golden rule: do unto others as you would have them do unto you. Similarly, the principle of sowing and reaping is alive and well in business. Be aware of the seeds you are sowing, as that is surely what you will reap.

Ethics and integrity are of supreme importance to your start-up business. By using sound business practices based on good ethics, you will give yourself another boost in your pursuit of success. You will attract like-minded employees and customers. High integrity is the best and easiest way to run your business.

Business Ethics and Integrity Summary

- Having a reputation for integrity and ethics will serve your business in many ways.
- Ensure that you and your staff operate with honesty and integrity.

Rule #3

ROLES AND RESPONSIBILITIES

Rule #3

Successful start-ups have personnel with well-defined roles and responsibilities.
Start-up failures have conflicts about the roles and responsibilities.

Former president Ronald Reagan had a philosophy that he did not care who got the credit as long as the goal was met. You should run your business the same way. You and your business team members are all striving for the same end goal. Don't get hung up on titles and be mindful that you are using the strengths of each team member. People should work to their strengths, and it should be clear which person is responsible for which activity.

In our business, we each brought our experiences and business strengths (and weaknesses) to the company. My partner was an excellent financial manager and organizer. He naturally gravitated to that part of the business. It was clear from the beginning that he was the go-to guy when it came to matters of finance: lines of credit, equipment financing, insurance, etc. It was equally clear that my role was to manage and cultivate the relationships of our customers and suppliers. That was my background and experience. It worked well because we were not competing for the same role within the company.

> ### Case Study
>
> I gave an example earlier that explained that we had to raise more money in our second year of business. That job was clearly my partner's and not mine. We issued more stock and raised more money. There was never any question about who would undertake that task. My role was to grow the sales of our company and to develop our supplier base. My partner's role was to manage our finances. As much as possible, you should have members of your team whose talents are different but complementary to yours.

The flip side of this coin is that in the infancy stage of the business, the owners do whatever tasks and jobs they have to do make the company run. Duties and tasks may overlap in the early stages of the business, but responsibilities don't overlap. Entrepreneurs do whatever it takes to make the business succeed. It may not be your role to work in packaging or warehouse, but if you can't afford to hire people for these tasks then you will have to do them—in addition to your primary role.

As your business grows, your role will naturally evolve. In the early years, everyone in the business is a producer that is maximizing revenues and outputs. Later roles evolve and you may become more of an administrator or organizer and begin to implement systems that run the business. As you begin hiring managers to run the systems and functions of the business, one of your toughest challenges will be to let go of enough control to allow your expanded team to be effective. This is one of the main problems I see with growing businesses. You must be willing to delegate enough authority to enable the company to continue to grow.

> Tasks and duties
> may overlap, but
> responsibilities do not.

Tasks versus Responsibilities

It is important to have a clear understanding of who is responsible for what in the business. You can certainly ask for and receive help to complete a particular task in the business, but ultimately the responsibility is yours. For example, I would often take another member of our management team with me to make a presentation to an important customer, but the responsibility for securing that business was mine. You can share the task but not the responsibility.

Once your managers are in place and effective, your role will be more of a leader or visionary than a doer or manager. This is also the stage in which many entrepreneurs sell their companies. Over the ten years of building our company and prior to the sale of our business, we each became proficient in the other's area of expertise to some degree but never left our primary roles.

In the early years of your business, the various functions and departments will run on the expertise and competence of its people. Later, the company will have more systems in place and it will be less reliant on people knowledge. I always think of McDonald's when I think of a business with systems. This global company has the same platform of effective systems that are easily understood and utilized by its often young and inexperienced workforce, whether it is in a city in the United States or on the other side of the world. Its systems are uniform throughout the world. Strong systems allow the company to operate at optimal efficiency.

Resist the action of putting the wrong people into the wrong roles. Your brother-in-law having an accounting degree doesn't mean he should be your accountant. Financial and legal help is expensive for a small business, but the end result of short-changing these areas can be disastrous. Robert Kiyosaki, the best-selling author of the *Rich Dad Poor Dad series*, relays the story of the high price he paid by not protecting the idea and his business for the Velcro® surfers wallet. It wasn't long before the idea (product) was duplicated and stolen. Without patent protection from a qualified attorney, his company was vulnerable.

The same advice applies equally to financial advice. You should seek the counsel of a finance person versed in small business issues, preferably start-ups. These highly paid professionals do not have to be employees but they should be on your team. Your team members and their roles should be clearly defined. You will want to use this information in your presentation to bankers and investors.

If you determine that you have the wrong person in the wrong role at your company, do not be timid about making a change. I've never heard the leader of a company say that he fired someone too soon. You are in business to make a profit and serve your customers. Having the wrong person in the wrong job can be damaging to your business if left unchecked. This applies to all levels of the company. A friend of mine who started a medical products company was able to grow the company to a healthy $25 million in sales per year. At that point, he had the objectivity to step back and realize that he was not the best person for the role of president. He hired someone as president whose skill set is allowing the company to grow to the next level. You must know your strengths and weaknesses as well as your employees.

> ### Case Study
>
> As a manufacturing company, one of the most critical roles in our company was the production manger. Soon after the launch of the business, we had performance and attendance problems with our production manager. It became apparent that we had to replace him. He was not the right person for the job and his performance was below what we expected and needed. His replacement brought a whole new energy and manufacturing expertise to our business. It was at that point that we (the owners) could begin to focus less on production and more on sales and strategic parts of the business. Production/operations was now under control and we could go about the important work of building our business.

These errors resulting from personnel mistakes usually must be corrected at a later date and with significantly more costs attached to them. Be thoughtful and demanding in your selection of the business team. If you make a mistake in the personnel area, acknowledge it, correct it quickly, and move on.

Start-up failures also fail to hire the right-type people. The right-type people are those who are the best at what they do and are relentless in their pursuit of being the best. If you are starting a software company and need to build a sales team, don't be satisfied with salespeople who are content to go home at 5:00 p.m. without closing the deal. Find that one in ten persons who simply won't rest until the deal is done. Early-stage businesses tend to be people-dependent so put effort into finding the right people and putting them in the right roles with specific responsibilities. This will make the business more effective and efficient.

Roles and Responsibilities Summary

- Roles and responsibilities will evolve but will not fundamentally change over time as your business grows.
- You must ensure that you hire the right people to take over various roles and responsibilities, and you must learn to delegate to your staff.
- Start-up successes will have the right people in the right jobs.

Rule #2

YOUR AREA OF EXPERIENCE AND EXPERTISE

Rule #2

> **Start-up successes start businesses inside their "area of expertise."**
> **Start-up failures start business in areas where they are not expert.**

Start-up successes are launched by entrepreneurs who have had prior experience and success in the business or market of their new venture. Start-up failures are launched by entrepreneurs who do not have prior experience in the business they are starting. They are forced to learn the fundamentals of the business as they launch and deal with normal start-up issues.

This "area of expertise" distinction is one of the most important—*period*. It is a primary reason why so many start-up businesses fail. It is fundamentally important that you invest your time, your money, and especially other people's money in an area where you have some level of expertise. The "area of expertise" distinction is one of the most crucial to lowering your start-up risk.

One of Warren Buffet's basic investing principles is this: don't invest in something that you don't understand. Warren Buffet would choose to invest in the Coca-Cola Company over a high-tech company any day. He could understand and appreciate the value and business fundamentals of Coke.

> ### Case Study
>
> Robert Kiyosaki (author of *Rich Dad Poor Dad*) tells about his dad who, after years of working in Hawaii's public school system, decided to open an ice cream shop. This was a business he knew very little about, and, as simple as it seemed on the outside, every business has its challenges. The new venture ultimately went out of business, causing much heartache and financial loss.

The founders of start-up successes have experience in the specific business or industry they are starting. Having knowledge about the specifics of a business can make a huge difference when challenges arise. If you know your business or industry well, you will have contacts within the industry, and this can be invaluable to you in times of need. You will have relationships with suppliers, consultants, and customers.

For example, one tactic we used with two suppliers is that we negotiated extended payment terms. This was extremely important when cash flow became tight. Our payable terms went from thirty days to sixty days. We were able to do this because we had a personal and business relationship with people at both these suppliers. This simple tactic helped our cash flow tremendously. Now we were being paid by our customers in approximately thirty days but paying two of our largest suppliers in sixty days. Later, we took this one step further and offered our large customers a discount for paying early. We offered a 2 percent discount if they paid within ten days. Several of our large customers took us up on this since it was a great deal for them. At that point, we were being paid in ten days and paying our vendors in sixty.

If you did a research project on the reasons that well-funded start-ups go out of business, this *experience* distinction would be at or near the top of the list. Michael Ames in his book *Small Business Management* gives as his number one reason for business failure the "lack of experience." This experience factor is key to your success. Take time to learn the business and market.

> **Case Study**
>
> Several years ago I had an opportunity to buy an on-going bed-and-breakfast in Florida. As much as I love the beach and would like to own a B&B near a beach in Florida, I would never jump into that business without first working at a B&B—for a year or two. Nothing can take the place of experience in the business—nothing.

All this is not to say that you can only launch a business that you have worked in, but it does mean that you should understand the business thoroughly. If you are considering starting a business outside your area of expertise, make every effort to gain some real experience in the business. Hire people with experience in your business. Take the time to learn the business from the inside whenever possible. You will learn details of the business that you will never see from an outsider's perspective.

This experience factor is one reason franchises are so popular. Franchises offer the support and expertise stemming from years of success. There is a price for this in the form of fees and profit sharing, but using the expertise of the franchise brand can be your best option if you are venturing into an unknown business.

If you start your business outside your area of expertise, you begin your journey with an uphill battle. You will be well served by working for a company in your chosen industry and gaining that irreplaceable experience and knowledge.

Your Area of Expertise Summary

- Your area of expertise is defined as a business you have experience in already.
- Having an area of expertise offers you contacts, relationships, and other noncash currency that can assist you with your business.
- If you choose a business outside your area of expertise, consider a franchise operation.

The next chapter discusses the most important factor in start-up success: determination.

Rule #1

SUCCESS THROUGH DETERMINATION

Rule #1

> **Start-up successes have 100 percent faith and determination to be a success.**
> **Start-up failures often give up just before success comes.**

Somewhere along the path of starting a new business, a leap of faith will be required. Faith is a very powerful force. It is a pillar of religion. It is a pillar of the entrepreneur. One thought that seems to be a truism in the world of the entrepreneur is this: take the leap and then the net will appear. The net won't appear until you leap. That is, you can't see it until you need it. This conviction of faith is crucial to your success. The feeling of faith can be bolstered by a solid plan, by the right financing, by the right management team, and by mitigating your risk. But you won't be able to cover every contingency and every "what-if" scenario. At some point, you will need the faith in yourself and your plan and make the jump. Start-up successes have 100 percent faith and determination to be successful.

> Take the leap and
> the net will appear.

Mental toughness is another key requirement of the entrepreneur. You will hear from naysayers telling you that you must be crazy to start a business. The economy is too bad, consumer spending is down, credit is too tight, and on and on. Usually these people don't have your best interest at heart and you should avoid talking about your plans and business aspirations with them. You might be surprised to see that some of your closest friends and family members will be your biggest detractors. You must be mentally tough and sure of your road to overcome these types of obstacles. Your determination to make your business succeed will serve you well as you are tested in the early years of your business.

Case Study

Robert Kiyosaki, author of *Rich Dad, Poor Dad*, tells of his early years in business when he was forced to actually live in his car. Mr. Kiyosaki had a single-mindedness to be successful in his business. Even in the midst of that low point of his business life, he had the mind-set of success. It is fair to say that his mental toughness and determination were amazing. He had a burning desire for success. Giving up was never a consideration or option for him.

Start-up failures are missing the iron-clad faith and determination to be a success. They don't have that burning desire to make their start-up a success. They often give up just before success arrives. They are unsure of their plan and their faith waivers.

When the time comes for your *leap*, realize that you won't know all the answers. Of course you will have done all the market and customer research, prepared your plans, checked off the "Top 10 Distinctions" here, but you still won't know everything. Don't get bogged down in research and plans. Don't get paralyzed and neglect the leap. Educated guesses are just fine! Don't let *perfect* get in the way of *good*.

Have faith in yourself and your plan. Vince Lombardi said, "Winners never quit and quitters never win." I've known business people who gave up too early. Often the greatest triumphs come soon after a great defeat. You simply cannot give up just because things get tough. If starting a business was easy, everyone would do it. It is the fact that it is not easy that makes the end result worth the effort. If it was easy, the reward wouldn't be as great. Remember to never, ever, ever give up.

Determination Summary

- With faith and preparation, your business can minimize risks and be a success.
- Keep going, even when things are tough.

AFTERWORD

As you go through the "Top 10 Rules," my hope is that you will use them as a checklist. You can eliminate much of the risk of starting a business if you learn from entrepreneurs who went before you. Risk elimination in each of the key business areas will help ensure your success.

Give yourself every opportunity for success by launching a business that you are experienced with. Give that business a solid dose of equity financing, couple that with sales that exceed the plan and expenses that are under control, mix in key personnel with integrity who take ownership for their areas of expertise, watch your cash-flow model, and work your line of credit. With your iron-clad determination to have a successful business, nothing can stop you.

Why This Book?

If you ask most seasoned entrepreneurs if they are risk takers, their answer would be no.

Entrepreneurs have the courage to take calculated risks but as a group are not risk takers in the common sense of the phrase. Entrepreneurs take *managed risks*. And there is a big difference between a blind risk and a managed risk. The purpose of this book is to help you learn from successful entrepreneurs and manage the risks like they do so that when you start your new business it won't be risky at all.

We need more entrepreneurs. Being an entrepreneur is being one of the most valued people in society. Entrepreneurs create jobs; they contribute to the economy; they put food on the tables of their employees; they contribute to the growth and well-being of their communities and their countries; they pay taxes. Ronald Reagan once said, "Entrepreneurs and their small enterprises are responsible for almost all the economic growth in the United States." This statement still holds true today. Small businesses generated 60 percent to 80 percent of the new jobs over the last decade, according to the Small Business Administration. The SBA also says that they produce thirteen times the number of patents per employee compared with large firms. Sba.gov/advo.
In this economic downturn, we need more entrepreneurial activity. According to the SBA, new business starts since 2005 have been declining. What better time to start your business than now, when large companies across the country are laying people off? Many of today's finest companies were started during an economic downturn—Disney, Microsoft, Hewlett-Packard, Oracle, Cisco, and Allstate Insurance, to name a few. The engine of our economy is small business.

Financial Freedom

In pursuit of your financial freedom, you don't have to *get a job*. Getting a job and working at the will of someone else may be one of the riskiest decisions you can make, especially today. How many people do you know who worked loyally for a company for years—if not decades—only to find themselves unemployed as soon as the economy softened? They lost their source of income through no fault of their own. Given today's economic climate, when layoffs or reductions in force (RIFs) are common, you may find yourself at more risk by leaving your employment in the hands of someone else.

With your own business, you have control. When you work for somebody else, he or she has control—control over your livelihood, your income, and your peace of mind. If you will learn how to be an entrepreneur and learn how to lower the risk of starting a business, your financial future will be much more secure than relying on someone else to *give* you a job. Because if he *gives* you a job, he can always *take* that job away.

Once you learn the skill set of successful entrepreneurs, you can use that knowledge to attain financial security. You will be in control of your finances—from top to bottom.

Business Climate

Contrary to what politicians say, the government does not "create jobs." Governments and politicians confiscate and spend other people's earned money. The best any government can do is to do no harm—stay out of the way and create a low-tax and low-regulation environment that encourages business and the entrepreneur. No matter what your political preference is, most people want to see a healthy level of business activity, trade, growth, and job creation. The evidence is irrefutable: economic systems that have a low amount of government interference perform best for all citizens and raise the standard of living for everyone.

In the United States, we live in a predominately capitalist economic system. The means of production and economic activity are privately owned. You can be part of that ownership. You can choose to be an entrepreneur, to work for yourself, and to build a company that can directly benefit hundreds or thousands of people, not to mention the multiplying benefits to other companies from which you will buy and sell products and services. Successful businesses are welcomed in their communities and help build their local economy, and in turn they help the economy of the nation as a whole.

The great economies and great countries of the world were built by entrepreneurs and visionaries—men and women who had vision and foresight and took risks. Perhaps the ultimate start-up risk was taken by our founding fathers when they started this country by declaring their independence from England. I can't think of a riskier or more successful start-up.

I have one last thought to leave with you. This country was built by great individuals from our founding fathers who decided to start a new country to the early industrialists and entrepreneurs who took risks and paved the way for future growth. It is a great virtue to be a capitalist and an entrepreneur. Capitalism has provided the highest standard of living for more people than any other economic system ever created.

Consider this:

- The fruits of your labor and new business will positively impact your community and in turn our whole country.
- You will bring benefits to your fellow man by providing jobs in your community.
- You will bring benefits to your employees by allowing him or her to provide for his or her family and contribute to his or her sense of well-being and self-sufficiency.
- You will bring benefits to other companies through the materials, supplies, and services your business will purchase. In economics, this is called the multiplier effect. Your business dollars go out into the world and create more value, wealth, jobs, and business activity.

- You will bring benefits to churches and charitable organizations by creating wages and income for you and your employees to donate as they wish.
- You will bring benefits to the government by paying taxes and reducing the number of unemployed.
- You will build a solid and financially secure future for yourself and family.

I often have conversations with good friends who think it is "too risky" to start a business. These conversations take place in an economic climate of job cuts and slow economic growth where that person is fearful of losing his job. But which is more risky: to work for a company and a boss who can downsize you—*reduction in force* as it is commonly called—at a moment's notice or to develop a solid business plan and control your own livelihood? In this economy, I would rather take my chances on my own and control my own destiny. If you own your own successful company, no one will ever lay you off. Your job security is locked up for good.

One last reason for you to *mind your own business* is that once you learn the successful skills of the entrepreneur, you can literally control your own financial destiny. At some point you will want to retire. In order for you to retire, you must have built up enough *passive* income so that it is higher than your expenses. Passive income is income you don't have to work for. This is the opposite of *earned* income or W-2 income. With passive income, the money continues to come in regardless of whether or not you work. If you build a solid company with good people, you can achieve a steady stream of passive income. If you build your company with competent people, they can run it even in your absence.

Entrepreneurship and capitalism should be held in the highest regard. Being an entrepreneur is a noble profession and is needed now more than ever. It is my sincere desire that, by following the distinctions outlined here, you will be empowered to begin or further your entrepreneurial journey with your risks drastically reduced.

Here's to your business success through managed risk!

GLOSSARY

area of experience and expertise: The specific business that you are an expert in or that you have the most passion for.

balance sheet: Shows a financial picture of a business. It specifically shows assets, liabilities, and ownership. It is measured at a given point in time—like at year-end.

cash-flow statement: Shows how cash is exchanged between the business and the outside world. It shows how cash is generated and what it is spent on.

debt financing: Money put into a company in the form of a loan. This money is a debt for the company and is paid back out of cash from business activities.

equity financing: Money or capital that is invested into a business in exchange for ownership in the business. This money is not a loan; it is repaid in the form of stock, dividends, and profit sharing.

entrepreneur: A person who creates value and profit by contributing to the betterment of society through the creation of a business by the allocation and risk of resources for the enrichment of himself and his employees.

guerrilla marketing: Utilizing a variety of traditional and nontradtional communication methods to reach your target audience.

income statement (profit and loss statement): Measures expenses against sales revenue to show the income (or loss) to a business. It is measured over a specific period of time—like a month or year.

joint venture: A formal arrangement of value exchange between two companies where the new company gives up equity/ownership in exchange for an investment from its JV partner.

line of credit (LOC): A prearranged loan from a lending institution that you pull from and pay back regularly in order to manage cash flow.

selling effectiveness procedures (SEPs): A system of work instructions for sales and marketing activities used to standardize the sales process into simple, effective, and accountable procedures.

unique selling proposition/business niche: A statement, much like a business's mission statement, that defines the factor(s) that differentiate the sales offering of the company—marketing to your target audience what differentiates your company's offering from all others.

BIBLIOGRAPHY

Business Start-Up Resources

Berkery, Dermot. *Raising Venture Capital for the Serious Entrepreneur*. New York: McGraw-Hill, 2007.

Gerber, Michael E. *The E-Myth Revisited: Why Most Small Businesses Don't Work and What to Do About It*. New York: HarperCollins, 1995.

www.gobignetwork.com is a start-up funding site.

Sales Resources

Revenue generation and sales effectiveness:
www.revenueconsultant.com

Business and sales effectiveness—audio books, CDs, and DVDs
www.nightingale.com

Business Education Resources

Keys to Success: The 17 Principles of Personal Achievement. Edited by Matthew Sartwell, based on Napoleon Hill's "*Think and Grow Rich*".

The TAO of Warren Buffett. Buffet, Mary, and David Clark. New York: Scribner, 2006.

Rich Dad, Poor Dad. New York, NY: Business Plus, 2010 (Robert Kiyosaki books and games).

Start with Why. Sinek, Simon. New York, NYPortfolio Hardcover, 2009.

Balance Sheet Basics: Financial Management for Nonfinancial Managers. Spurga, Ronald C. New York, NYPenguin Group, 2004.

ABOUT THE AUTHOR

Brian Davies

Mr. Brian Davies has been in the medical device industry for 25 years. He was co-founder of PCI Technology, an OEM contract manufacturing company that was sold to Brady Corporation (NYSE: BRC) in 2006. In 2005 PCI was recognized by the *Dallas Business Journal* and SMU Cox School of Business as one of Dallas' Fastest 100 Growing Companies. PCI, / Brady Medical, now Strukmyer Medical, provides wound dressings and other disposable medical devices to companies worldwide. Strukmyer Medical (Brady Medical) currently operates in a new 53,000 sf facility in Dallas, Texas, where Mr. Davies served as General Manager and Vice President of Sales.

Currently, Mr. Davies is Founder and Vice President of BioMed Laboratories, Llc. BioMed is a FDA registered and ISO certified medical contract manufacturing company. This successful start-up company is engaged in the manufacture of medical and personal care products in tubes, bottles, and jars. These products (such as antibiotic ointments) are sold into the professional healthcare and consumer markets.

www.biomedlabs.com

Throughout his career Mr. Davies has held various positions of responsibility including, Planning, Customer Service, Sales / Sales Management, and Mergers and Acquisitions, and General Management. Mr. Davies holds BSBA and Master of Science degrees.

Mr. Davies is also a successful real estate investor with income producing properties in Texas and Florida.

www.ingramcontent.com/pod-product-compliance
Lightning Source LLC
Chambersburg PA
CBHW021004180526
45163CB00005B/1894